TENOR SAXOPHONE
BOOK ONE

Band Expressions Author Team

Co-Lead Author: Robert W. Smith

Co-Lead Author: Susan L. Smith

Michael Story   Garland E. Markham   Richard C. Crain

Contributor: Linda J. Gammon

Percussion Contributor: James Campbell

Editor: Thom Proctor

Consulting Editor: Patrick Roszell

Art Credits: page 5, *Butterfly II* by Paul Giovanopoulos, ©1995 Paul Giovanopoulos c/o Theispot Showcase;
page 34, *Scenes of Daily Life in Korea* by Kim Junkeun, ©Christies Images Ltd. 1995;
page 38, *Celebration 1975* by Charles Searles, ©Smithsonian American Art Musuem, Washington D.C./Art Resource, NY.

UNIT 1

The Art of Playing

Instrument and Parts

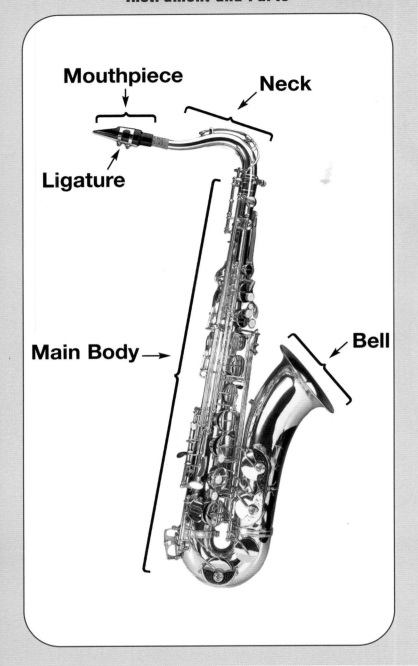

Mouthpiece

Neck

Ligature

Main Body →

Bell

Assembly Procedure

1. Place the reed in your mouth as you assemble your instrument.

2. Loosen the neck screw and gently twist the neck into the main body of the instrument, being careful not to bend the octave key. Tighten the neck screw.

3. Place the mouthpiece onto the neck and adjust it to the proper place, being careful not to tear the cork.

4. Place the ligature on the mouthpiece before inserting the reed and tightening the ligature screws.

5. Use a small amount of cork grease as necessary

Disassembly Procedure

1. Remove the ligature and reed from the mouthpiece. Store the reed in a reed guard.

2. Remove the mouthpiece and wipe it out before storing it in the case.

3. Remove the neck, swab the entire instrument and wipe off the outside of the keys

4. Place the instrument carefully in the case and close all latches completely.

5. Cases are for your instrument only, not for music, folders, or books.

Care and Maintenance

- Keep the tenor saxophone clean and free of moisture by swabbing after each use.

- Gently wipe the outside of the keys with a soft cloth each time before storing it in the case.

- Wash out your mouthpiece with lukewarm, soapy water once a week.

- Always remove the reed from the mouthpiece each time and store it in a reed guard.

- Avoid standing your tenor saxophone against a chair when not in use.

- Take your instrument to a professional shop once a year for maintenance.

Rest Position

Ready Position

Play Position

Posture and Hand Position

- Sit toward the front of the chair with your feet flat on the floor.

- Position your upper body so that it is straight and relaxed as if you were standing.

- Adjust your neck strap so that it supports the weight of the instrument and allows you to keep your head up.

- Place your fingers comfortably over the key pearls and close to the keys. Press your right thumb up under the thumb rest.

- Place your elbows comfortably away from your body.

Embouchure Formation

1. Rest your upper teeth on the top of the mouthpiece about 1/4" from the tip.

2. Cover your lower teeth with your lips and form the embouchure.

3. Point your chin, firm the corners of your mouth, and hold your lips and cheeks close to the teeth.

4. Check with a mirror.

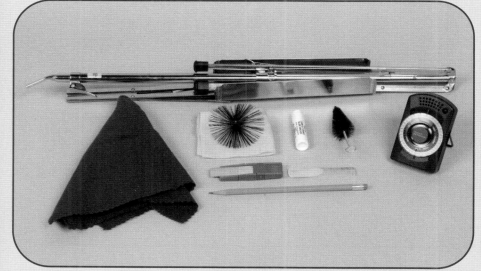

Supplies

- Cloth swab
- Soft Cloth
- Reed guard with several reeds
- Mouthpiece brush

- Cork grease
- Metronome
- Pencil
- Mirror
- Wire music stand

UNIT 1 WILL BE PRESENTED BY YOUR TEACHER

Creative Tools of Music (Units 2 and 3)

Articulation—a slight interruption of the air stream with the tongue

Bar Line—a vertical line placed on a staff to divide music into measures

Breath Mark—a recommended place to breathe

Clef—placed at the beginning of the staff to identify the note names

Embouchure—the natural formation of the facial and lip muscles on the mouthpiece or reed

Fermata—hold the note or rest longer than note value

Final Bar Line—indicates the end of a piece of music

Flat—lowers the pitch of a note one half step

Grand Staff—treble and bass clef staves joined together

Interval—the distance between two pitches

Ledger Lines—short lines placed above or below the staff

Measure—the space between two bar lines to form a grouping of beats

Musical Alphabet—the letter names of the notes used in music

Rhythm—the organization of sound and silence in time

Sharp—raises the pitch of a note one half step

Staff—5 lines and 4 spaces on which notes are placed

Time Signature—a symbol placed at the beginning of the staff indicating the number of beats per measure and what kind of note gets one beat

4/4 4 beats per measure
quarter note receives one beat

Musical Alphabet Games

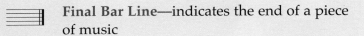

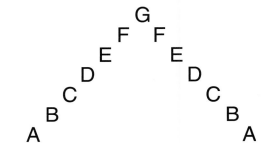

Air Stream   Inhale   E x h a l e   Inhale
(1 2 3 4)   (1   2   3   4)   (1 2 3 4)

Band @ Home

LESSON 1

1. Teach one or more of your family members how to inhale and exhale in order to play a wind instrument.
2. Time how long you and your family members can exhale against a piece of paper.

LESSON 2

1. Demonstrate to your family the following:
   • Instrument assembly
   • Rest/Ready/Play positions
   • Instrument disassembly
2. Complete the Instrument Parts and Assembly Procedure worksheet and bring it to our next class.

LESSON 3

1. Practice assembling and disassembling your instrument.
2. Create a variety of rhythms to sing with the recording of "One Note Rock" using the syllable "toh" or "doh." **CD :4**

G

Butterfly II, by Paul Giovanopoulos

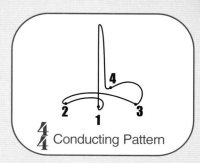

$\frac{4}{4}$ Conducting Pattern

1 First Sounds

Set   Ready ' Breathe
1   2   (3   4)

G ⟶

2 Mouthpiece Rock

Play two times

Set   Ready ' Breathe
1   2   (3   4)

G ⟶   Rest   '   G ⟶   Rest   '

1 2 3 4 1 2 (3 4) 1 2 3 4 1 2 (3 4)

CD :5

3 First Note

Set   Ready ' Breathe
1   2   (3   4)

CD :6

4 One Note Shout

Play two times

Set   Ready ' Breathe
1   2   (3   4)

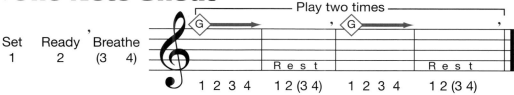

Rest   Rest

1 2 3 4   1 2 (3 4)   1 2 3 4   1 2 (3 4)

CD :7

5 One Note Reggae

Set   Ready ' Breathe
1   2   (3   4)

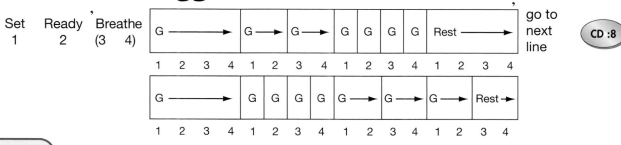

go to next line

CD :8

G ⟶	G ⟶	G ⟶	G	G	G	G	Rest ⟶
1	2	3	4	1	2	3	4	1	2	3	4	1	2	3	4

| G ⟶ | | | | G | G | G | G | G ⟶ | G ⟶ | G ⟶ | Rest ⟶ |
| 1 | 2 | 3 | 4 | 1 | 2 | 3 | 4 | 1 | 2 | 3 | 4 | 1 | 2 | 3 | 4 |

Band @ Home

LESSON 1

1. Practice "Mouthpiece Rock" with the recorded accompaniment.

2. Demonstrate for your family how to produce the first sounds on your mouthpiece.

3. Perform "Mouthpiece Rock" with the accompaniment track for your family.

LESSON 2

1. Practice forming your embouchure. Remember—it is important that you practice bringing the mouthpiece to your embouchure to become more comfortable with producing these first sounds.

2. Sustain your first tone on G as long as possible while keeping the air stream and tone steady. Be sure to focus and "energize" your air stream.

3. Perform "One Note Shout" with the accompaniment track for your family and/or friends.

LESSON 3

1. Sustain a steady sound over 8 to 12 counts.

2. Practice your first note and articulation by playing "One Note Reggae." Practice your "toe-tap" with a steady beat while articulating the quarter notes.

3. Show your family and/or friends the graphic *Butterfly II* and explain the groupings of "4." Perform "One Note Reggae" for your family and/or friends and read *Butterfly II* as your music.

4. Create your own graphic that represents patterns of quarter notes and quarter rests.

UNIT 4

Creative Tools of Music

Critique—an evaluation of the quality of a performance

 Fermata—hold the note (or rest) longer than the note value

Intonation—the accuracy of pitch or pitch relationships in the performance of music

Ledger Lines—short lines placed above or below the staff for pitches beyond the range of the staff

 Rest—a silent unit of time.

Soli—a line of music played by a small group of instruments

Tutti—all play

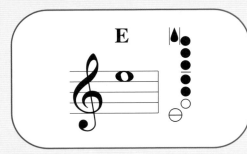

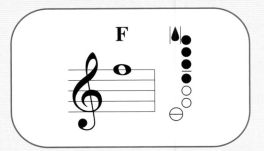

- Light blue highlights indicate new notes.
- Light yellow highlights indicate new rhythms.
- Light red highlights indicate new terms and symbols.

$\dfrac{4}{4}$ = 4 beats in a measure

Quarter note gets one beat

6 Learning Our First Note

Quarter note = ♩ = 1 beat

Quarter rest = 𝄽 = 1 beat

7 Quarter Note Rock CD :9

8 Fermata Warm-Up CD :10

9 More Quarters CD :11

6

10 **Soli Jam** CD :12

11 **My Quarters**

12 **New Notes**

13 **El Toro** CD :13

Band @ Home

LESSON 1

1. Practice "More Quarters" for our next lesson. This exercise will help you develop your music reading skills.

LESSON 2

1. Schedule a consistent, daily time for practice in a quiet place so you are not distracted and can focus entirely on your music.

2. Practice "New Notes." This exercise introduces two new notes for your instrument. Notice the fingering chart in your book for the new notes.

3. Play "New Notes" for your family to show them what you have been learning.

4. Compose your own piece on the line entitled "My Quarters" in your book. Use any combination of quarter notes and quarter rests on your first note for the eight-measure composition. Be prepared to perform your composition in our next class.

LESSON 3

1. Practice "Mixing the Three" in Unit 5.

2. Explore www.band-expressions.com to find out more information about music and your instrument.

UNIT 5

Creative Tools of Music

Canon—a technique to compose music in which the melody is introduced in one voice and echoed by another voice

Solo—a performance by one person playing alone, with or without accompaniment

14 *Mixing the Three*

15 *Solo Rock* CD :14

Solo   tutti

16 *Creative Expression*

   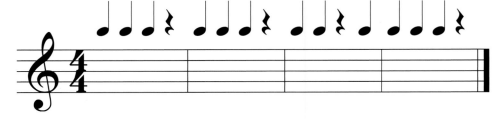

17 *Going the Distance*

18 *Hymnsong* CD :15

19 *Putting It Together*

20 **Round and Round We Go**

21 **Canon Roll**

Creative Tools Notation

Band @ Home

LESSON 1

1. Remember—it is important to follow our daily practice routine.

2. Practice "Going the Distance." This challenging exercise reviews what we have already learned.

LESSON 2

1. Practice "Putting it Together." This selection reviews what we have learned to this point.

2. Remember the importance of the daily practice routine to build endurance.

LESSON 3

1. Compose and teach a family member a canon using body percussion.

2. Be prepared to teach your canon to the band in our next lesson.

3. On the "Creative Tools Notation" line, practice drawing your clef, time signature, barlines, quarter notes and rests, a fermata, and a final barline.

Creative Tools of Music

Balance—all parts played and heard equally

Duet—a piece of music with two interacting parts

Harmony—the result of two or more tones sounded at the same time

Key—the tonality of a piece of music

Key Signature—flats or sharps placed at the beginning of the staff that indicate which notes are to be altered throughout the piece

March—music for a parade or procession

Musical Line—direction or shape of a musical thought or idea

Unison—all performers play the same note

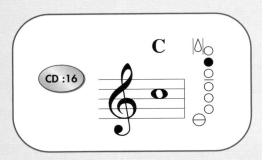

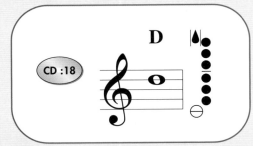

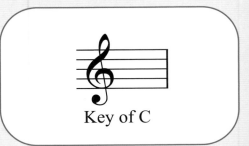

22 Three Note Warm-Up

23 Woodchopper's Ball   CD :17

Words and Music by
JOE BISHOP and WOODY HERMAN

24 Two for the Show (Duet)

25 Two Tone Workout

26 Woodchopper's Ball (C Version)   CD :19

Words and Music by
JOE BISHOP and WOODY HERMAN

27 A "Rock" Nophobia (Duet)
(The Eentsy Weentsy Spider)

Traditional, U.S.A.

28 Heroes March (Duet) CD :20

March

29 Balance Our Sound (Duet)

30 Ode to Joy (Duet) CD :21

LUDWIG VAN BEETHOVEN, Germany

Band @ Home

LESSON 1

1. Practice playing the new note we learned today.

2. Perform "Woodchopper's Ball" with the accompaniment CD for your family and friends.

LESSON 2

1. Play the new note for your family. Demonstrate your ability to hold and control steady long tones/beats.

2. Play 'Heroes March' with the CD accompaniment for your family and friends.

LESSON 3

1. Practice long tones on C and D. Play both of these notes for four counts with four beats of rest between these two pitches.

2. Perform "Ode to Joy" with the accompaniment track for your family and friends.

3. Explore www.band-expressions.com to discover more information about music and your instrument.

Creative Tools of Music

Chorale—a slow, "hymn-like" composition

Composer—a person who writes music

Phrase—a musical sentence or statement

 Repeat sign—symbol that indicates to go back and play the section of music again

PORTRAIT

John Williams

One of the most popular and successful American orchestral composers of the modern age, John Williams is the winner of five Academy Awards, 17 Grammys, three Golden Globes, and two Emmys. Mr. Williams has composed the music and served as music director for nearly eighty movies, including "Jaws;" "E.T.: The Extra-Terrestrial;" "Hook;" the "Indiana Jones;" trilogy and the "Star Wars" series. He is the Laureate Conductor of the Boston Pops Orchestra, which he conducted for 13 years and currently holds the title of Artist-in-Residence at Tanglewood, Massachusetts. He may be best known for the music he has written for the Olympics, including the well-known "Olympic Fanfare."

Whole note	= o	= 4 counts
Whole rest	= ▬	= 4 counts

Half note	= ♩	= 2 counts
Half rest	= ▬	= 2 counts

31 Echo Warm-Up

32 Whole Lotta Fun

33 Half the Time

34 Thanksgiving Song

Folk Song, England

35 Celebration CD :22

Words and Music by
RONALD BELL, CLAYDES SMITH, GEORGE BROWN, JAMES TAYLOR, ROBERT MICKENS, EARL TOON, DENNIS THOMAS, ROBERT BELL and EUMIR DEODATO

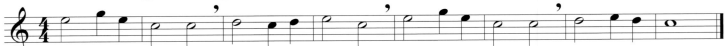

36 Whole Note Warm-Up

37 Phrase Phun

38 *OK Chorale (Duet)*

39 *All Through the Night*

Folk Song, Wales

40 *Augie's Great Municipal Band (Duet)* CD :23

Music by
JOHN WILLIAMS

This Arrangement © 2003 Bantha Music   All Rights Reserved

41 *Theme From "Jaws"*

Music by JOHN WILLIAMS

This Arrangement © 2003 Universal - Duchess Music Corporation   All Rights Reserved

42 *Creative Expression*

Band @ Home

LESSON 1

1. Practice playing a whole note followed by a whole rest on each of the five notes we have learned so far.

2. Practice playing a half note followed by a half rest on each of the five notes.

3. Practice "Celebration" with the accompaniment.

LESSON 2

1. Practice the melodies we learned today.

Try to play two measures before taking a breath to create a phrase.

2. Time how many seconds you can sustain a note while maintaining a steady sound.

LESSON 3

1. Practice the song "Jaws."

2. On line 42, compose your own shark song using the notes you have learned so far. Experiment with soft and loud and fast and slow to create different types of sharks. What type of shark are you?

3. Perform the shark song you create for your family and friends. You may have the opportunity to perform your song for the class in our next lesson.

4. Ask your family or friends to name a piece by John Williams. If they do not know any of his works, tell them about the music you heard or played in class. (Star Wars, Jaws, E.T., etc.)

5. Perform "Augie's Great Municipal Band" and "Jaws" for your family and friends.

UNIT 8 IS PRESENTED BY YOUR TEACHER

Creative Tools of Music

Anacrusis—one or more notes that occur as a lead-in to the first full measure

Dynamics—musical performance levels of loud and soft

Sight-reading—reading and performing a piece of music for the first time

Subdivide—dividing a note into smaller sections or fractions

Dynamic Markings

p	the symbol for piano, meaning to play soft
mp	the symbol for mezzo piano, meaning to play medium soft
mf	the symbol for mezzo forte, meaning to play medium loud
f	the symbol for forte, meaning to play loud

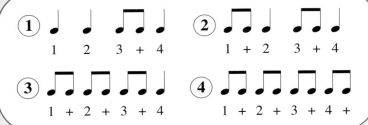

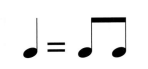

43 Playing the Phrase CD :24

44 Reading the Eighths

45 Three Pairs and a Caterpillar

46 Rain, Rain Go Away CD :25

Traditional

47 Creative Expression

48 Feel the Force! CD :26

mf   *f*   *p*   *mf*   *f*

49 Chitty, Chitty Bang Bang CD :27

Words and Music by
RICHARD M. SHERMAN and ROBERT B. SHERMAN

f   *mf*   *f*   *mf*   *f*

50 Arre, Mi Burrito! CD :28

Folk Song, Latin America

51 Juba

African-American Folk Song, U.S.A.

52 Mary's New Groove CD :29

Traditional, U.S.A.

53 Duerme Pronto CD :30

Folk Song, Spain

54 Long Legged Sailor

Traditional, Folk Song

55 Bang the Drum All Day CD :31

(I Don't Want to Work)

Words and Music by TODD RUNDGREN

I don't want to work, just want to bang on the drum all day.

I don't want to work, just want to bang on the drum all day.

This Arrangement © 2003 WARNER-TAMERLANE PUBLISHING CORP. All Rights Reserved

Band @ Home

LESSON 1

1. Remember to follow your warm-up procedure. Play one of your favorite songs from earlier in the book to complete your warm-up.

2. On the Creative Expression line, create and notate four measures of eighth note and quarter note combinations using any pitch you can read and play. Clap, count, and play your composition.

3. Practice "Rain Rain, Go Away" with the CD accompaniment.

LESSON 2

1. Play the new song "Juba."

2. Draw dynamic symbols (piano, forte, mezzo forte, and mezzo piano) where you think they belong.

3. Play "Juba" with the dynamics you have added. Be prepared to play this in class next time.

4. Memorize "Rain, Rain Go Away."

LESSON 3

1. Teach the words to "Bang the Drum All Day" to your family and friends. Invite them to perform "Bang the Drum All Day" with you and the accompaniment track.

Creative Tools of Music

Melody—a series of musical tones that form a recognizable phrase

Ostinato—a repeated melodic or rhythmic pattern

Slur—a curved line placed above or below two or more notes to indicate that they are to be performed smooth and connected

Tempo—the speed of the beat

Tie—a curved line connecting two notes of the same pitch and played as if they were one

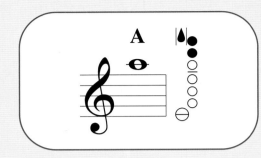

A

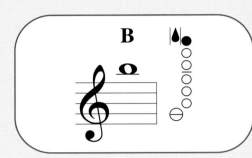

B

Tie   Slur

PORTRAIT

Percy Grainger
(1882–1961)

An Australian composer, he lived from 1882 to 1961. His music is based on folk songs he collected from throughout the British Isles. He used a phonograph to record men and women singing the songs that were passed down to them from their parents and grandparents. In his arrangements of these folk songs for band, he tried to keep the phrasing as close to the original vocal performance as possible.

56 *New Vistas*

57 *Claire de Lune* CD :32

Folk Song, France

58 *Mary With My New Notes*

Traditional, U.S.A.

59 *Los Pollitos* CD :33

Folk Song, Ecuador

60 *When the Saints Go Marching In* CD :34

JAMES M. BLACK and
KATHERINE E. PURVIS, U.S.A.

61 **Catch a Falling Star** CD :35

Words and Music by
PAUL VANCE and LEE POCKRISS

This Arrangement © 2003 EMILY MUSIC CORPORATION and MUSIC SALES CORPORATION   All Rights Reserved

62 **Sarasponda**

Folk Song, Holland

63 **Shepherd's Hey** CD :36

Country Dance, England

Band @ Home

LESSON 1

1. Complete "Mary With My New Notes" by notating the missing melody. We will play our completed song in our next lesson.

2. Practice playing "Claire De Lune" with the accompaniment track.

LESSON 2

1. Practice "Los Pollitos," "When the Saints Go Marching In," and "Catch a Falling Star" at different tempi.

2. Explain and play for someone at home the difference between a tie and a slur.

3. Revise "Mary With My New Notes" looking for:

   • Straight note flags
   • Neatly written note heads
   • Correct notes
   • Evenly spaced notes

4. Add the following to your composition:

   • New appropriate words
   • Dynamics

5. Be prepared to share your composition with the band.

LESSON 3

1. Create a one measure rhythmic ostinato to accompany "Mary With My New Notes".

2. Your ostinato should be on our first note (G) using any combination of quarter and eighth notes and quarter rests.

3. Remember that an ostinato is a repeated pattern.

Creative Tools of Music

> **Accent**—play the note with more emphasis

Chord—three or more tones sounded at the same time

♩. **Dot**—increases the value of the preceding note or rest by one half

1st and 2nd Endings—play the first ending the first time only and the second ending the second time

3/4 **Time Signature**—a symbol placed at the beginning of the staff with the top number indicating that there are 3 beats per measure, and the bottom number indicating a quarter note, which equals one beat

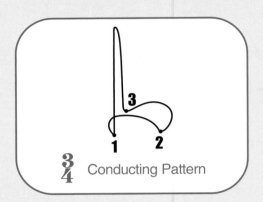

3/4 Conducting Pattern

PORTRAIT

Gustav Holst
(1874–1934)

Gustav Holst was born in Cheltenham, England in 1874 and began composing while at Cheltenham Grammar School. While studying at the Royal College of Music, he met Ralph Vaughan Williams, another famous composer, and the two were close friends, always playing drafts of their newest compositions to each other. Holst was a teacher his whole life and because of a heavy and demanding teaching load, it took him many years to write his most famous work, "The Planets" (1914-1916). Despite his initial training at the Royal College of Music, Holst was largely self-taught as a composer, mostly learning by experience. He was an intense nationalist, and after his rejection from the Royal military because of his bad eyesight, he became a conductor of the military band, and toured much of Europe supporting the British through music. Some of his most well-known pieces include "Moorside Suite," "Suite in Eb," "Suite in F" and "The Planets."

64 Three at a Time

65 Batman Theme **CD :37**

Words and Music by NEAL HEFTI

66 Around Her Neck
She Wore a Yellow Ribbon

Traditional, U.S.A.

67 Shusti Fidli CD :38

Folk Song, Czechoslovakia

68 Change the Drum CD :39

69 Oh Dear,
What Can the Matter Be? CD :40

Folk Song, England/Scotland

70 In the Bleak Midwinter CD :41

GUSTAV HOLST, England

Band @ Home

LESSON 1

1. After warming up properly, practice "Batman Theme" and "Around Her Neck."
2. Perform these songs for your family and friends. You may wish to ask your family if they remember "Batman Theme" from the classic television series.

LESSON 2

1. Explain 3/4 time to one of your family members.
2. Ask them to count for you as you play "Shusti Fidli."
3. Practice conducting each exercise before performing.

LESSON 3

1. Create and notate a new 8-count accent pattern. Be prepared to notate the pattern on the board during our next lesson for the band to play.
2. Practice "Oh Dear, What Can the Matter Be?" and "In the Bleak Midwinter."
3. Teach one of your family members how to conduct in a 3/4 time signature. Ask the family member to conduct as you play "Oh Dear, What Can the Matter Be?"

Creative Tools of Music

Accidental—a sharp, flat or neutral, in a way not indicated in the key signatures

Concert pitch—the actual sounding pitch of a note played by an instrument

Introduction—a short section of music preceding the piece

Natural—this symbol cancels a previous sharp or flat sign; like a flat or sharp, it is used for the entire measure

Rock—a style of popular music that originated in America, characterized by a strong rhythmic beat and electronic instruments

Concert Pitch	F	D	E♭	B♭
C Instruments	F	D	E♭	B♭
B♭ Instruments	G	E	F	C
E♭ Instruments	D	B	C	G
F Instruments	C	A	B♭	F

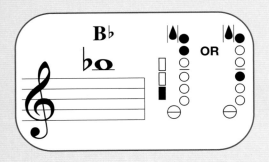

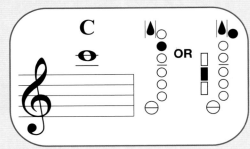

71 *Song in E Flat*

mp

72 *There's No One Exactly Like Me*

By BETTY ANN RAMSETH

73 *March Flam* CD :42

74 Happy Birthday to You! CD :43

Words and Music by
MILDRED J. HILL and PATTY S. HILL

75 Jingle Bells CD :44

J. PIERPONT, U.S.A.

76 Jingle Bell Rock CD :45

Rock!

Words and Music by
JOE BEAL and JIM BOOTHE

77 Sunrise, Sunset CD :46

Lyrics by SHELDON HARNICK
Music by JERRY BOCK

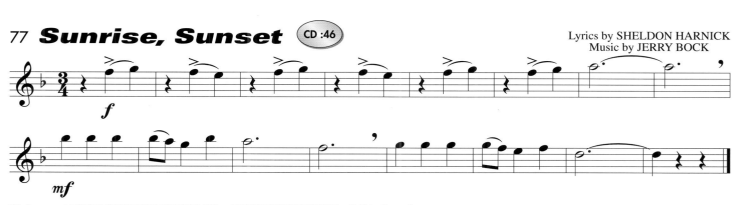

78 Hine Ma Tov CD :47

Folk Song, Israel

Band @ Home

LESSON 1	LESSON 2	LESSON 3
1. Practice "There's No One Exactly Like Me" and "Happy Birthday to You!" 2. Perform "Happy Birthday to You!" for your family and friends.	1. Practice "Jingle Bells" and "Jingle Bell Rock" alone and with the accompaniment tracks. 2. Memorize "Happy Birthday to You!"	1. Practice playing long tones on the notes in your Concert Pitch Grid. 2. Practice playing concert pitches with a friend from band or while someone plays the concert pitches on the piano or keyboard.

Creative Tools of Music

Balance—the dynamic strength and importance given to instruments/voices within a composition

Multiple Measure Rest—a symbol indicating more than one measure of rest

3 **Rehearsal Numbers/Letters**—markings above the staff that indicate specific locations in the music

Sight-reading—the playing of a piece of music for the first time

Style—how notes, rhythms, and articulations are treated in musical performance

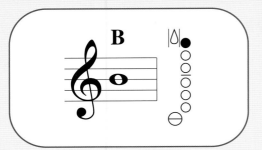

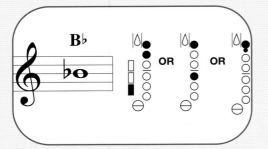

SIGHT-READING PROCEDURE MAP (SRPM)

1. Look at the title, composer, time signature, and key signature.

2. Look through the entire piece for the musical road map and for any key or time signature changes.

3. Follow along each line of music with your finger to be sure you know all of the notes and understand all of the rhythms and musical markings.

4. Count through the entire piece silently while tapping your foot.

5. Finger/airstick through the entire piece. Be sure to look at the words and symbols around the notes for all of the performance information.

6. Silently practice the difficult passages.

79 *Lotta Latin*

80 *Feliz Navidad* CD :48

Words and Music by JOSE FELICIANO
Arranged by MICHAEL STORY

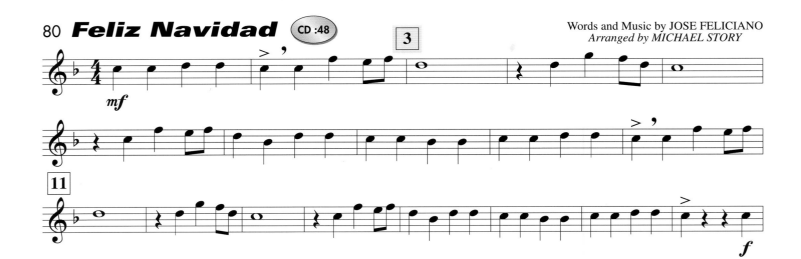

Line 80 continued

81 *Up on the Housetop* CD :49

BENJAMIN RUSSELL HANBY, U.S.A.
Arranged by MICHAEL STORY

82 *Rock Warm-Up*

83 *Winter Wonderland* CD :50

Words by DICK SMITH
Music by FELIX BERNARD
Arranged by ROBERT W. SMITH

84 *Holiday Warm-Up*

85 We Wish You a Merry Christmas

Traditional, England
Arranged by ROBERT W. SMITH

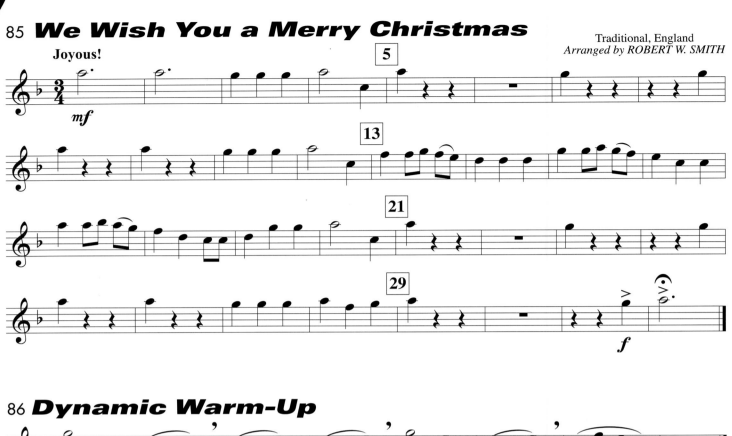

86 Dynamic Warm-Up

87 African Patapan   CD :51

Carol, France
Arranged by MICHAEL STORY

88 Concert Chorale

Auld Lang Syne (Solo)

Traditional, Scotland

Jingle Bells (Solo)

J. PIERPONT, U.S.A.

<table>
<tr><td>

Band 🏠 Home

UNIT 13

LESSON 1

1. Practice "Feliz Navidad."

2. Warm-up slowly and carefully on long tones before each practice session.

LESSON 2

1. Practice "Feliz Navidad" and "Up on the Housetop," considering the style for each piece.

2. Remember to isolate the more difficult passages, playing them slowly and gradually increasing the speed.

3. Record yourself playing your part on "Feliz Navidad." Write down what you discovered from critically listening to yourself play.

</td><td>

Band 🏠 Home

UNIT 14

LESSON 1

1. Review all three of the concert pieces, striving for individual improvement.

2. Make a recording of your performance of each piece and turn it in at our next lesson. Your teacher will review your recording and provide feedback for improvement.

LESSON 2

1. Review all of the concert pieces we have learned so far. If you are having difficulty with particular sections of a piece, play the section slowly to improve before going on.

</td><td>

Band 🏠 Home

UNIT 15

LESSON 1

1. Review all of the concert pieces.

LESSON 2

1. Polish your performance on all of the concert pieces and prepare all music, equipment, and concert attire.

2. Tell your family and friends the reporting time and concert time.

3. Practice the solo pieces, "Jingle Bells" and "Auld Lang Syne," and perform them for your family and friends.

</td></tr>
</table>

UNITS 16—18 WILL BE PRESENTED BY YOUR TEACHER

Creative Tools of Music

UNITS 16—18 ARE PRESENTED BY YOUR TEACHER

Allegro—fast tempo

Andante—slow (walking) tempo

Moderato—moderate or medium tempo

89 New Horizon Warm-Up

mf

90 Finger Stretch

mf   *p*   *mf*   *p*   *f*   *p*   *mf*   *f*

91 Marianne   CD :52

Lively!

Folk Song, Jamaica

mf   >>>   *f*

92 Scooby-Doo, Where Are You?   CD :53

With energy!

Words and Music by
DAVID MOOK and BEN RALEIGH

mf

This Arrangement © 2003 Warner-Tamerlane Publishing Corp., Music Sales Corporation and Chappell & Co. All Rights Reserved

93 Over There   CD :54

March

Words and Music by
GEORGE M. COHAN

mf

1.   2.

This Arrangement © 2003 WARNER BROS. PUBLICATIONS U.S. INC. and EMI FEIST CATALOG INC. All Rights Reserved

94 The Chicken Dance   CD :55

(a/k/a Dance Little Bird)

By TERRY RENDALL and WERNER THOMAS

mf   *f*   *mf*   *f*

This Arrangement © 2003 INTERVOX MUSIC All Rights Reserved

95 Walking Waltz

Andante

1.   2.

mf

96 Moderato March

97 Go, Go, Allegro!

98 Can Can

JACQUES OFFENBACH, France

99 Creative Expression

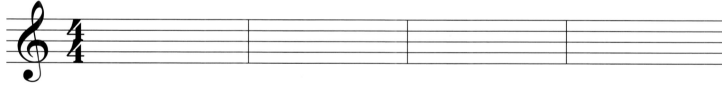

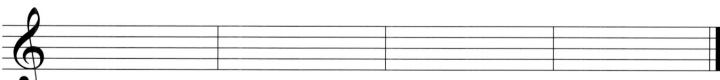

Band @ Home

LESSON 1

1. Practice "Marianne" and "Scooby Doo, Where Are You?" with the accompaniment CD.

2. Perform "Marianne" and "Scooby Doo, Where Are You?" for a family member or friend. Ask them if they have heard these songs before and if so where.

LESSON 2

1. Practice "Over There" and "The Chicken Dance."

2. Make up new appropriate motions to "The Chicken Dance" and teach them to someone in their family.

LESSON 3

1. Practice "Can Can" at Moderato, Allegro, and Andante tempi.

2. Explain the different tempi to one of your family members and perform "Can Can" at those tempi.

3. Create an 8-measure rhythmic composition on the staff provided and then apply the tempo markings you have learned in this lesson—Moderato, Allegro, and Andante. Perform your composition using a selected note.

UNIT 20

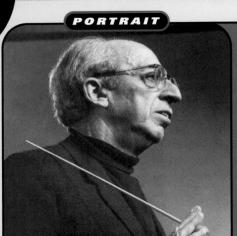

PORTRAIT

Aaron Copland
(1900-1990)

Aaron Copland composed musical works for ballets, orchestras, choirs, and the movies. He composed "Billy the Kid" and "Rodeo," music based on American folklore. He also composed "Lincoln Portrait," which was a tribute to President Abraham Lincoln. One of Copland's best-known works is "Fanfare for the Common Man."

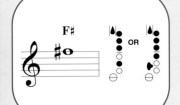

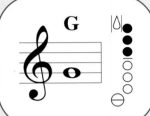

Key of G

100 *Siren Warm-Up*

mf

101 *Great Granddad*

Cowboy Song, U.S.A.

Allegro

mf

102 *Git Along Little Dogies*

Cowboy Song, U.S.A.

Moderato

1. 2.

mf *f*

10 *mf*

18

103 *Goodbye Old Paint*

Cowboy Song, U.S.A.

Allegro

f

9

104 *Shaker Hymn*

Appalachian Folk Song, U.S.A.

Andante

mf

Line 104 continued

105 *Five Foot Two, Eyes of Blue*

Lyric by SAM LEWIS and JOE YOUNG
Music by RAY HENDERSON

Allegro

f

106 *The Hey Song*   CD :59

By MIKE LEANDER and GARY GLITTER

Rock

f

11

107 *New for a Few*

Andante

mf

108 *Norwegian Mountain Dance*

Folk Song, Norway

Allegro

mf

109 *The Merry Go Round Broke Down*   CD :60

Words and Music by
CLIFF FRIEND and DAVE FRANKLIN

Allegro

f

1.   2.

110 *Creative Expression* **Complete the Composition Worksheet #13.**

Band @ Home

LESSON 1

1. Perform the three selections learned today, "Git Along Little Dogies," "Great Granddad," and "Goodbye Old Paint," for your family.

LESSON 2

1. Practice the new note we learned today, concert E.

2. Play "Shaker Hymn" for your family. Ask if they have heard this song before.

3. Tell your family that Aaron Copland used "Shaker Hymn" in his composition "Appalachian Spring."

4. Play "The Hey Song" with the accompaniment track.

LESSON 3

1. Perform, "Norwegian Dance", and "The Merry-Go-Round Broke Down" for your family and friends.

2. Complete Worksheet #13, "110 Creative Expression."

Creative Tools of Music

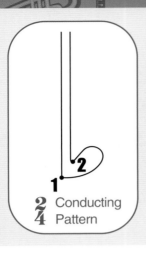

Mariachi Cobre

𝄌   **Measure Repeat Sign—** a symbol that indicates to repeat the previous measure

2/4   **Time Signature—** 2 beats per measure Quarter note receives one beat

𝄾   **Eighth Rest—** receives 1/2 beat

2/4 Conducting Pattern

111 *Back to Home*
Andante

mf

112 *Getting Even*
Moderato

mf

113 *Cucu Cucu*
Folk Song, Spain

Allegro

mf

114 *Cielito Lindo*   CD :61
Folk Song, Mexico

Allegro

f

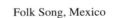

115 *Building the Long Tone*
Moderato

mf

116 *Eighth Rest Workout*
Moderato

mf

117 *Mi Caballo Blanco*
Folk Song, Chile

Moderato

mf

118 Rest on the Beat

119 El Juego Chirimbolo CD :62

Folk Song, Ecuador

120 Relay Game

121 San Sereni

Folk Song, Latin America

122 La Cucaracha

Folk Song, Mexico

123 El Relicario CD :63

Folk Song, Mexico

124 Creative Expression

Band @ Home

LESSON 1	LESSON 2	LESSON 3
1. Continue to practice, striving for the very best tone quality you can from your instrument.	1. Practice "Eighth Rest Workout" and "Rest on the Beat."	1. Practice "San Sereni," "La Cucaracha," and "El Relicario."
2. Play "Cielito Lindo" and "Cucu Cucu" for your family and friends.	2. Play "El Juego Chirimbolo" for your family and friends.	2. Continue to strive for the very best tone quality as you practice and perform.
		3. On line 124 write a song using the following: 2/4 time signature, eighth notes and rest, repeat sign, and any of the pitches we have learned so far.

Creative Tools of Music

Legato—smooth and connected without interruption between the notes (soft start, long duration)

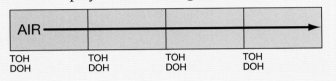

AIR

TOH DOH   TOH DOH   TOH DOH   TOH DOH

Staccato—play the note lightly and detached (light start, short duration)

AIR

TOH   TOH   TOH   TOH

Tenuto—play full value (long duration)

AIR

TOH DOH   TOH DOH   TOH DOH   TOH DOH

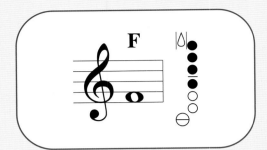

F

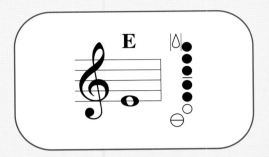

E

125 Theme From "The Surprise Symphony"   CD :64

FRANZ JOSEPH HAYDN, Austria

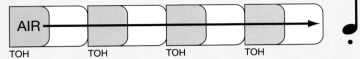

Moderato

126 Song of the Volga Boatmen

Folk Song, Russia

Andante

127 Paradiso   CD :65

By ROBERT W. SMITH

Gently

128 Smooth Sailing

Andante

129 **Dance of the Reed Flutes**

PETER ILYICH TCHAIKOVSKY, Russia

130 **The Long and Short of It**

131 **Sea Chanty** CD :66

Traditional Sea Chanty, England

132 **Can Can**

JACQUES OFFENBACH, France

133 **Wipe Out** CD :67

By THE SURFARIS

This Arrangement © 2003 MIRALESTE MUSIC and ROBIN HOOD MUSIC CO.   All Rights Reserved

Band @ Home

LESSON 1

1. Practice staccato articulations on all of the notes you have learned. It will take daily practice to train the muscles necessary to play articulations.

2. Warm-up slowly and carefully on long tones before each practice session.

3. Practice the "Surprise Symphony" with the accompaniment.

LESSON 2

1. Practice staccato and legato articulations on the notes you have learned. Practice slowly and carefully using the exact tonguing method needed for each articulation style.

2. Sight-read "Sea Chanty" as an example of legato and staccato style.

LESSON 3

1. Practice playing staccato, legato, tenuto, and slurs on each of the notes you have learned. Improvise with each articulation style on any exercise we have played so far and decide which articulation sounds the best. It will take daily practice to develop the muscles necessary to produce these varying articulations and styles.

2. Be sure to warm-up slowly and carefully on long tones or slow dexterity exercises before each practice session.

Creative Tools of Music

Scenes of Daily Life in Korea, by Kim Junkeun

Crescendo—gradually get louder.

Decrescendo—gradually get softer.

Largo—very slow tempo

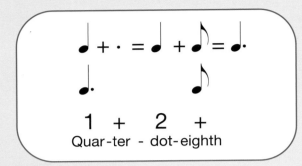

19th Century, ©Christie's Images Ltd. 1996

134 Louder and Softer

135 Ouma

CD :68

Mother Horse and Colt

Folk Song, Japan

136 Sakura

Cherry Blossoms

Folk Song, Japan

137 Kaeru No Uta (Duet)

Folk Song, Japan

138 Pentatonic Warm-Up

139 Dots
Moderato

140 Ha'kyo Jung CD :69
Andante
Folk Song, Korea

141 Hua Gu Ge
Andante
Folk Song, China

142 Arirang
Andante
Folk Song, Korea

143 Dotted Note Warm-Up
Andante

144 Largo From "The New World Symphony"
Largo
ANTONÌN DVORÀK, Czechoslovakia

145 Crescent Moon
Moderato
Folk Song, China

146 Creative Expression Compose a pentatonic melody and rhythm accompaniment on Worksheet #16.

 **Band @ Home**

LESSON 1

1. Practice the pieces we played today, working to improve the articulations and crescendo and decrescendo. Practice slowly and carefully, remembering to use the exact tonguing method needed for each articulation style.

LESSON 2

1. Practice the "Pentatonic Warm-up" and "Arirang." Make a recording of both of these for review. Feedback on your progress will be provided.

2. You will turn in your recording of "Arirang."

LESSON 3

1. Practice and perform your favorite pieces of Asian music we studied this week.

2. Complete Worksheet #16, 146 Creative Expression.

3. Practice your composition and be prepared to perform for the class.

UNIT 24

Creative Tools of Music

Da Capo (D.C.)—return to the beginning   Fine—the end

PORTRAIT

George Gershwin
(1898–1937)

George Gershwin's songs are some of the most lasting modern popular music written in the 20th Century. George Gershwin died when he was still fairly young. He is credited with being one of the first composers to merge jazz and classical music styles. One of his most famous works is the folk opera "Porgy and Bess."

147 *Low Tone Warm-Up*

148 *Register Change Exercise*

149 *Golden Gate March*
Moderato

150 *'S Wonderful* CD :70
Flowing

Music and Lyrics by
GEORGE GERSHWIN and IRA GERSHWIN

151 *Rhapsody in Blue*™ CD :71
Flowing

By GEORGE GERSHWIN

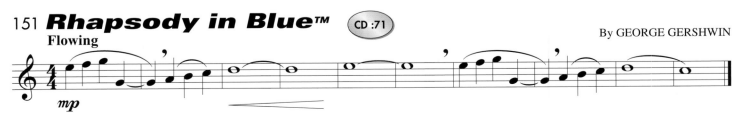

UNIT 24

152 The Donkey Song

Traditional, U.S.A.

153 Summertime CD :72

By GEORGE GERSHWIN, DuBOSE and DOROTHY HEYWARD and IRA GERSHWIN

This Arrangement © 2003 GEORGE GERSHWIN MUSIC, IRA GERSHWIN MUSIC and DuBOSE AND DOROTHY HEYWARD MEMORIAL FUND   All Rights Reserved

154 I Got Rhythm CD :73

Music and Lyrics by
GEORGE GERSHWIN and IRA GERSHWIN

This Arrangement © 2003 WB MUSIC CORP.   All Rights Reserved

155 Creative Expression/Arrange and Notate
Arrange and notate on Worksheet #17.

Band @ Home

LESSON 1

1. Practice "Rhapsody in Blue" and "'S Wonderful."
2. Practice your low notes and the "Register Change Exercise."

LESSON 2

1. Practice "Summertime" and "Donkey Song."
2. Practice your "Register Change Exercise."

LESSON 3

1. Practice "Summertime" and "I Got Rhythm" with the accompaniment tracks.
2. Complete Worksheet #17, 155 Creative Expression.

37

Creative Tools of Music

Drum Circle—an interactive group of people gathered in a circle to play music on percussion instruments; a facilitator who directs the group in rhythm activities and improvised patterns usually leads a drum circle

Ritardando (Rit.)—gradually slow down

Syncopation—rhythm with the emphasis or stress on a weak beat or weak portion of a beat

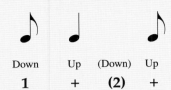

Down	Up	(Down)	Up
1	+	(2)	+

Celebration, by Charles Searles (b. 1937)

©Smithsonian American Art Museum, Washington, D.C., Art Resource, N.Y.

156 You're a Grand Old Flag CD :74

GEORGE M. COHAN, U.S.A.

157 Hill and Gully CD :75

Folk Song, Jamaica

Caribbean

158 Cheki, Morena

Folk Song, Puerto Rico

Spirited!

159 African Warm-Up

Marilli

Gently

160 Che Che Koolay CD :76

Singing Game, Ghana

161 The Rooster's Call

Folk Song, Liberia

162 Green Sally Up

Folk Song, U.S.A.
D.C. al Fine

163 Hello Lungile CD :77

Folk Song, South Africa

Lively!

164 Lil' Liza Jane

Dixieland

Words and Music by
COUNTESS ADA DELACHAU, U.S.A.

Band @ Home

LESSON 1

1. Practice "You're a Grand Old Flag" and "Hill and Gully" with and without the accompaniment tracks.

2. Create your own warm-up with syncopation and be prepared to share it with the band during our next class.

LESSON 2

1. Practice "Che Che Koolay" and "The Rooster's Call."

2. Describe a drum circle to several friends and/or family members and lead them in a drum circle performance. Find something resonant that sounds like a drum when played with your hands such as a box, can, or container.

LESSON 3

1. Practice "Green Sally Up" and "Hello Lungile."

UNIT 26

IS PRESENTED BY YOUR TEACHER

Creative Tools of Music

Jazz—music rooted in improvisation and characterized by syncopated rhythms

𝄋 **Dal Segno (D.S.)**—repeat from the sign

Improvisation—the process of spontaneously creating a new melody

Swing—a style of jazz music characterized by the "lengthening" of the eighth notes that are on the beat

PORTRAIT

Edward Kennedy "Duke" Ellington
(1899-1974)

Duke Ellington is remembered as one of the greatest jazz artists and important composers of the Twentieth Century. He wrote thousands of compositions, which included jazz music, sacred music for the church, show music, and music for movies. Mr. Ellington composed jazz classics such as "It Don't Mean a Thing (If it Ain't Got That Swing)" and "Satin Doll." He was also a brilliant conductor, arranger, pianist, and bandleader.

165 Gentle Warm-Up

Gently

mp   *rit.*

166 Chorale

mp

167 Angel Band

African-American Folk Song, U.S.A.

Gospel

mf   *f*

168 Duke's Place
(a/k/a C Jam Blues)

Swing

Music by DUKE ELLINGTON
Lyrics by RUTH ROBERTS, BILL KATZ and ROBERT THIELE

Ba - by!   Take me   down to   Duke's Place.   Wild-est   box in   town is

Duke's Place.   Love that   pi - ano   sound in   Duke's Place.

169 New Note Warm-Up

170 Wade in the Water

Spiritual

African-American Spiritual, U.S.A.

171 It Don't Mean a Thing (If It Ain't Got That Swing)

Words and Music by
DUKE ELLINGTON and IRVING MILLS

Fine   D.S. ⅋ al Fine

172 Satin Doll

Swing

Music by DUKE ELLINGTON

Band @ Home

LESSON 1

1. Practice "Duke's Place" with the accompaniment track.

LESSON 2

1. Practice "Wade in the Water" and "It Don't Mean a Thing (If It Ain't Got That Swing)."

2. Play long sustained tones on your new notes.

LESSON 3

1. Practice "Satin Doll."

2. Improvise your own four-measure song using the notes concert F, E♭, and D. Be prepared to perform your improvisation for the class at our next meeting. Use the provided accompaniment track on your student CD.

CD :81

Creative Tools of Music

Half Step—the distance between two adjacent notes

Interval—the distance between two pitches

Scale—a stepwise progression used in melodies and harmonies

Whole step—a musical distance that equals two half steps

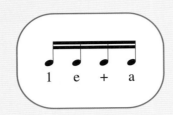

	W	W	H	W	W	W	H
	1	2	3	4	5	6	7	8
Concert Key	B♭	C	D	E♭	F	G	A	B♭
C Instruments	B♭	C	D	E♭	F	G	A	B♭
B♭ Instruments	C	D	E	F	G	A	B	C
E♭ Instruments	G	A	B	C	D	E	F#	G
F Instruments	F	G	A	B♭	C	D	E	F

173 There Are Many Flags in Many Lands
Traditional, U.S.A.

Flowing

mf

174 Oranges and Lemons
Folk Song, England

mf

175 Tinga Layo CD :82
Folk Song, Jamaica

Calypso

mf

176 Concert B♭ Scale Warm-Up

half step *half step* *half step* *half step*

1 2 3 4 5 6 7 8 7 6 5 4 3 2 1

177 Chester
WILLIAM BILLINGS, U.S.A.

mf ——— *f* ——— *mp* ——— *f*

178 Peep Squirrel CD :83
Folk Song, Africa

Mysterious

mf

f

179 Hao Peng You

Flowing

Folk Song, China

180 Kookabura

By MARION SINCLAIR

1 e + a 2 + 3 + 4 +

181 Ciranda   CD :84

Folk Song, Brazil

182 Over the Rainbow

Music by HAROLD ARLEN
Lyric by E.Y. HARBURG

Lyrical

Solo

A

Acc.

B

183 Creative Expression

Band @ Home

LESSON 1

1. Practice the "sizzle" breathing exercise. How long can you hold the sustain?

2. Practice "Oranges and Lemons" and "Tinga Layo." Perform them for your family and/or friends.

LESSON 2

1. Practice "Peep Squirrel."

2. Practice and memorize the concert B♭ scale.

LESSON 3

1. Count and play "Kookaburra" and "Over the Rainbow." Some students will have the chance to perform "Over the Rainbow" as a solo in the next band class.

2. On the line provided (183), create your own eight measure composition, using the key indicated and the rhythms and pitches you have learned so far.

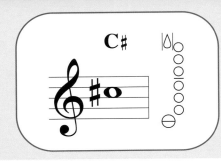

184 *Lip Slurs*

Moderato

185 *On the High "C's"*

Moderato

186 *Wabash Cannonball*

Traditional, U.S.A.

Moderato

187 *Matchmaker, Matchmaker*  CD :85

Lyrics by SHELDON HARNICK
Music by JERRY BOCK

Allegro

188 *Sleeping Beauty*

PETER ILYICH TCHAIKOVSKY, Russia

Allegro

189 *"B" Your Best*

Allegro

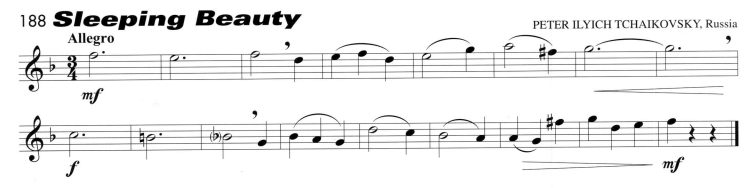

190 Theme From Ice Castles
(Through the Eyes of Love) CD :86

Music by MARVIN HAMLISCH
Lyrics by CAROLE BAYER SAGER

Andante

191 Concert C Major Scale

192 Santa Lucia

Folk Song, Italy

Moderato

193 Doo Wah Diddy Diddy CD :87

Words and Music by
JEFF BARRY and ELLIE GREENWICH

Moderato

194 The Hey Song CD :88

By MIKE LEANDER and GARY GLITTER

Allegro

11

Band @ Home

LESSON 1

1. Review the new note concert C you learned in this lesson.

2. Practice "Wabash Cannonball" and "Matchmaker, Matchmaker."

3. Ask your family and friends the name of the Broadway musical in which "Matchmaker, Matchmaker" was performed. ("Fiddler on the Roof")

LESSON 2

1. Perform "Theme from Ice Castles (Through the Eyes of Love)" for your family and friends. Ask if anyone has heard this song before and if so where.

LESSON 3

1. Practice the lip slurs introduced in class today. Be sure to make each note respond with the same quality and volume.

2. Perform "The Hey Song" in the new key for your family and friends.

3. On Worksheet #1, compose an 8-measure warm-up. You will have the chance to play this in class. This should contain some of the things we have discussed before that are contained in a good warm-up. This could include long tones, lip slurs, articulation exercises, and so on.

PORTRAIT

John Philip Sousa
(1854–1932)

Sometimes known as the "March King," John Philip Sousa wrote some of the most famous and recognizable marches in the world. Sousa was born in 1854 and he started studying music at the age of 6. When he was 13 years old his father enlisted Sousa in the Marines after he tried to run away from home to play in a circus band. In 1880, Sousa was appointed conductor of the United States Marine Band in Washington DC, which is known as "The President's Own." He later organized the Sousa Band and traveled the country presenting concerts with this organization. Throughout his illustrious career, Sousa wrote over 130 marches. In 1987, his "Stars and Stripes Forever" became the official march of the United States of America.

195 *More Lip Slurs*

196 *Caissons Go Rolling Along* CD :89

EDMUND L. GRUBER

197 *Marines Hymn*

Traditional, U.S.A.

198 *Anchors Aweigh* CD :90

Words and Music by
Capt. ALFRED H. MILES, U.S.N. (Ret.) and CHAS. A. ZIMMERMANN

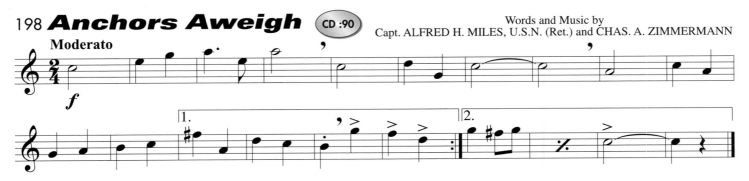

199 *El Capitan*

JOHN PHILIP SOUSA, U.S.A.

200 **The Thunderer**

JOHN PHILIP SOUSA, U.S.A.

201 **Blow Away the Morning Dew**

Folk Song, England

202 **The Yellow Rose of Texas** CD :91

Traditional, U.S.A.

203 **Na Na Hey Hey** CD :92

(Kiss Him Goodbye)

Words and Music by
GARY DE CARLO, DALE FRASHUER and PAUL LEKA

Band @ Home

LESSON 1

1. Always warm up with long tones and strive for the best tone quality possible.

2. Practice "Caissons Go Rolling Along," "The Marines Hymn," and "Anchors Aweigh."

3. Ask your family members if they can identify which branch of the U.S. Armed Services these marches represent.

LESSON 2

1. Remember to start your practice session with the proper warm-up.

2. Teach your family and friends about the composer John Philip Sousa.

3. Play "El Capitan" and "The Thunderer" for your family and friends.

LESSON 3

1. Practice "Blow Away the Morning Dew," "The Yellow Rose of Texas," and "Na Na Hey Hey (Kiss Him Goodbye)."

2. As you practice these three pieces, remember to play with the best sound possible, with the correct note values, and with the proper articulations.

Johann Sebastian Bach
(1685–1750)

Johann Sebastian Bach was one of the most important composers in European history. He was a church musician all of his life and people today still regularly sing and play his music in church. He did not play the piano until he was an old man, so most of his keyboard music was composed for the organ or clavichord, a very popular keyboard instrument during the Baroque era. The Baroque era style included much ornamentation that was added to clothing, furniture, and architecture. Baroque music also was very ornamented.

204 *Down and Up*
Moderato

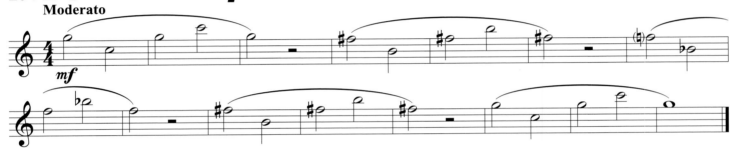

205 *Manhattan Beach* CD :93

JOHN PHILIP SOUSA, U.S.A.
Arranged by MICHAEL STORY

Moderate march tempo

206 Arirang CD :94

Folk Song, Korea
Arranged by MICHAEL STORY

207 Expressions in Blue CD :95

ROBERT W. SMITH

208 Bach Chorale

JOHANN SEBASTIAN BACH, Germany

209 Let Freedom Ring CD :96

Traditional
Arranged by ROBERT W. SMITH

Eine Kleine Nachtmusik

WOLFGANG AMADEUS MOZART, Austria

Over the Rainbow (Solo)

Music by HAROLD ARLEN
Lyric by E.Y. HARBURG

Music for the Royal Fireworks

GEORGE FRIDERIC HANDEL, Germany/England
Arranged by SANDRA DACKOW

Band @ Home

LESSON 1 & **LESSON 2**

1. Be sure to warm-up slowly and carefully on long tones before each practice session.

2. Review all of our concert pieces we have played so far.

3. Remember to isolate the more difficult passages, playing them slowly before gradually increasing the speed.

4. Make a recording of your performance of each piece and turn it in at our next lesson. Write down what you discovered from critically listening to yourself play. Your teacher will review your recording and provide feedback for improvement.

5. Practice the solos on page 50–51 "Over the Rainbow" and "Eine Kleine Nachtmusik," and perform them for family and friends.

UNITS 33–36
ARE PRESENTED BY YOUR TEACHER

RHYTHMIC REST PATTERNS

Concert B♭

Concert E♭

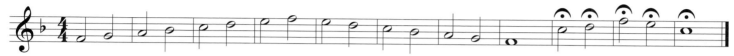

Concert F

Concert C

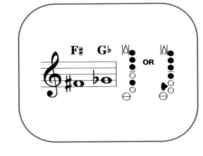

UNIT 22

UNIT 22

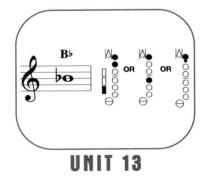

UNIT 20

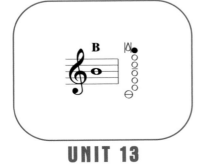

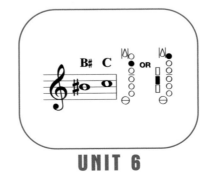

UNIT 20

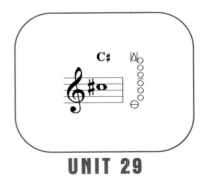

UNIT 13

UNIT 13

UNIT 6

UNIT 29

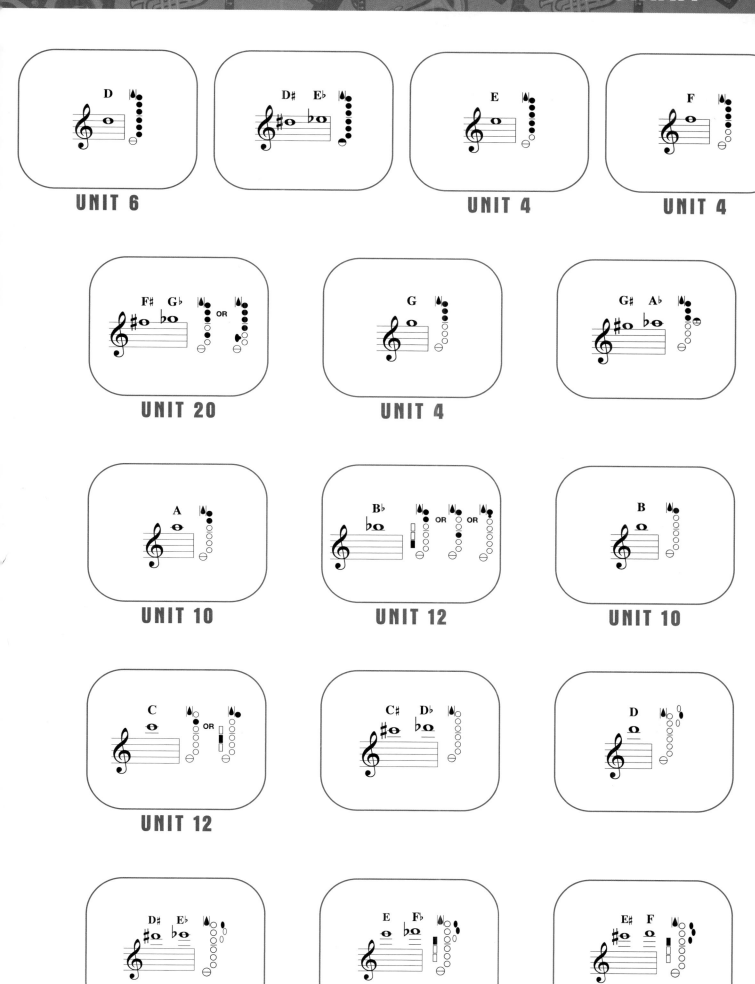

UNIT 6 **UNIT 4** **UNIT 4**

UNIT 20 **UNIT 4**

UNIT 10 **UNIT 12** **UNIT 10**

UNIT 12

Glossary

Page numbers refer to the Student Book page where the definition is shown.

1st and 2nd Endings—*Play the 1st ending, repeat the section and play only the 2nd ending the second time.* (18)

Accent—*Play the note with more emphasis.* (18)

♯, ♭, ♮ **Accidental**—*A sharp, flat, or natural not indicated in the key signature.* (20)

Allegro—*Fast tempo.* (26)

Anacrusis—*One or more notes that come before the first full measure.* (14)

Andante—*Moderately slow (walking) tempo.* (26)

Articulation—*A slight interruption of the air stream with the tongue.* (4)

Balance—*All parts played and heard equally. The dynamic strength and importance given to instruments/voices within a composition.* (10)

Bar Line—*The vertical line placed on a staff to divide the music into measures.* (4)

Breath Mark—*A recommended place to breathe.* (4)

Canon—*Music in which the melody is introduced in one voice and echoed by another voice.* (8)

Carol—*A song of praise or celebration.* (–)

Chorale—*A slow, "hymn-like" composition.* (12)

Chord—*Three or more tones sounded at the same time.* (18)

Clef—*A symbol placed at the beginning of the staff to identify the note names on the staff.* (4)

Common Time—*4/4 time signature.* (–)

Crescendo, Cresc.—*Gradually get louder.* (34)

Da Capo, D.C.—*Return to the beginning.* (36)

D.S.—Dal Segno—*Repeat from the sign.* (40)

Decrescendo, Decresc.—*Gradually get softer.* (34)

Dot—*Increases the value of the preceding note or rest by one half.* (18)

Duet—*A piece of music with two interacting parts.* (10)

Dynamics—*Musical performance levels of loud and soft.* (14)

Embouchure—*The natural formation of the facial and lip muscles on the mouthpiece or reeds.* (4)

𝄐 **Fermata**—*Hold the note or rest longer than note value.* (4)

Final Bar Line—*Placed on the staff to indicate the end of a piece of music.* (4)

Fine—*The end.* (36)

♭ **Flat**—*A symbol that lowers the pitch of a note one half step.* (4)

Folk Song—*A song of cultural heritage passed from generation to generation sometimes through aural tradition.* (–)

𝆑 **Forte**—*Loud.* (14)

Grand Staff—*The Treble and Bass Clef staves joined together.* (4)

Half Step—*The distance between two adjacent notes.* (42)

Harmony—*The result of two or more tones sounded at the same time.* (10)

Improvisation—*Spontaneously creates a new melody without the intent to revise.* (40)

Interval—*The distance between two pitches.* (4)

Intonation—*The accuracy of pitch or pitch relationships in the performance of music.* (6)

Introduction—*A short section of music at the beginning of a piece.* (20)

Jazz—*Music rooted in improvisation and characterized by syncopated rhythms.* (40)

Key—*The tonality of a piece of music.* (10)

Key Signature—*Flats and sharps placed immediately following the clef used to indicate which notes are to be altered throughout the piece.* (10)

Largo—*A very slow tempo.* (34)

Ledger Lines—*Short lines placed above or below the staff for pitches beyond the range of the staff.* (4)

Legato—*Smooth and connected without interruption between the notes.* (32)

March—*Music for a parade or procession.* (10)

Measure—*The space between two bar lines to form a grouping of beats.* (4)

𝄎 **Measure Repeat sign**—*A symbol that indicates to repeat the previous measure.* (30)

Melody—*A series of musical tones that form a recognizable phrase to express a composer's thoughts or statements.* (16)

𝆐𝆑 **Mezzo Forte**—*Medium loud.* (14)